Unsound

Also by Jennifer Martenson:

Xq28[1], Burning Deck 2001

Jennifer Martenson

Unsound

Burning Deck/Anyart, Providence

Acknowledgments:

Grateful Acknowledgment is made to the editors of the magazines in which versions of some of these poems have been published: *Columbia Poetry Review, How2, Insurance, New American Writing, No Roses Review, Ploughshares* and *Spoon River Poetry Review.*

"Preface," "Intimate Conversations," "Not Access But Exposure is Unlimited," and "Unsound," were published in *Re: Chapbook 4*, Reference Press, 1999.

"Xq28" was first published as a chapbook by Burning Deck in 2001.

"A Postcard from Aphasia" was printed as a broadside by Brass Door Press in 2002.

Burning Deck is the literature program of Anyart: Contemporary Arts Center, a tax-exempt (501c3), non-profit organization.

The cover reproduces Berenice Abbott's "Wave Pattern with Glass Plate," Cambridge, MA, 1958–61, by permission of Commerce Graphics, Ltd.

Unsound

Contents

Preface

In my attempt to explicate by touch, I struck my forehead violently against the corner of an ambiguity. Was I

holding your hand or merely an opinion? Here again were twisted paths, this time covered with damp, matted layers of perspective. Fate has a margin of error

equal in width to the desire of one woman for another, and the evidence is inadmissible at best, but still, this question may be grounds for prosecution. Granted: facts have roots. I get stuck where the tree provides merely

shade, not philosophical positions overgrown with brambles though my coat snags on the thorns. Closely wedged among surrounding concepts, intimacy would not move an inch from its negation. I had either to seek out a different gender or to climb across the blind-spot and resume my identity

on the other side. I reached for you as if for proof, knowing this would steer us straight into that guardrail meant to keep emotional entanglements from crossing over into physical desires. No sooner have I extricated

cause from correlation than I trip on a fault in the assumption. Sense goes numb immediately and the branch sways gently in the abstract.

Contact Sheet

"

We might begin subtracting

word from word, working our way

down to zero, though it won't provide

a clear view to the night in progress

any more than silence contradicts

the claim that what is not there can exert

a pressure on the eardrum. In the way that

metaphors are nested, one inside another,

surreptitiously. The task is to elucidate,

or disinter —

"

Her studious efforts to construct and maintain partitions
as between varieties of touch, which appeared as the blur
between affection and sexuality, were rigorous
in proportion to the real
absence of boundaries designated by these terms.
While the contrast was not sharp, it was
still painful. Like trying to pry physiology apart
from feeling: once again, a continuous geography
defying lines of latitude which had already dropped
below the threshold of mimesis and into a climate of censure
where, preliminary studies indicate, no light is safe.
Even if it's red. Or indirect. Exposure to harmful rays
may cause the arteries to constrict, reducing
the flow of meaning near the surface of the skin
to leave one feeling cold. Or near the surface of the sociopolitical
dispute regarding the constitutionality of certain acts
which may have more in common with cell division
than with decisions as to how to spend

It is true that touch need not involve the body. This does little to assuage
the failure of love to rhyme with love. In this dialect. I too am under orders

"

eyes' timbre / perishable / page still warm

as if / disintegrating inside nomenclature

barely recognizable / as if

                    in following

the path of speech / across a continent

or century

          degraded signal / acoustics

of error / filigree of saying and / not saying

writing / down and crossing out

                    another

relapse / each one memorized / and no

known cure / the progress of

erasure, once begun

                                                    "

an evening. Just as moral sanctions may have more to do with being
superimposed on grounds of economic privilege
than with denying this conflict of interests under oath.
Judging by recent trends in legislation, this dispute is likely to be vetoed
in favor of self-censorship and other defensive reflex actions
such as marriage. Or called off on account of a perfectly legal
resurgence of outright violence. Chemistry continues to improve
our ability to develop affectional biases into snapshots —
fixed early on in phrases such as "I feel so damn sick and dirty
I can't stand it anymore" — so neurotic even realism
can not compete. Even if the negative is
inverted, certain polarities — said to keep the world spinning
on it its axis, although fluctuations in its bias have been known about
for quite some time — remain in place, a sort of structural tenacity
having imprinted the psyche with a naturalization of the roles
we play and on which clarity — in fiction *and* biography —

---

to destroy all traces of the correspondence. Mispronunciations can be tragic.
What we must not say is what we reach across when the impossible begins

"

Wanting

to adhere, the letter is destined

to tear itself free, and even now is

shedding its precision

"

too heavily depends. Disobedience results in narrative
confusion: her hand trailing downward along her arm to grasp
her hand passed out of significance and into a tenderness
having neither code nor context. Which is not to suggest
a lack of tactility, merely the loss of meaning that occurs when,
having wandered off along a tangent to the plot, you get lost
in a fusion of pronouns and wind up at the convergence
of parallel lines, yourself the illusion. From which not the faintest
outline of a plot develops, even if the problem is left
soaking overnight. Or you get lost within the script by not being equivalent
to any of its characters. What to say? To whom?
On what occasion? Lying on the floor, suspended
between comfort and arousal, she traced consequences
in the rug. There was not enough light for an image
to form on the sticky layer of the possible. No solution
to the differentiation which had, by then, become chronic.

---

to leak. So it is also true that only the incomplete is permanent.

"

graphic

depictions of nothing / form of a wish / not

here not now / bequeathed to

an unnamed

so the interior is

counterfeit

conjecture / without benefit of

intonation / meet me / under the deletion

at / illumination's jagged edge

"

A Priori

*If sensation is only a word, what
becomes of the senses? (Sartre)*

SENSATION, A HYBRID NOTION She was very incisive as a teenager. She even began dissecting her own body **BETWEEN THE OBJECTIVE AND THE SUBJECTIVE** with words. And other sharp objects. The psychiatrist *(combining noises systematically)* said that she was most likely not a lesbian *(such devices were used sparingly)* but that nevertheless she had developed a dangerously symbiotic relationship with the girl whose name **CONCEIVED FROM THE STANDPOINT OF THE OBJECT AND** appeared as a scar *(conventionalized markings on stone, wood, metal, parchment, paper, or any other surface)* **APPLIED SUBSEQUENTLY TO THE SUBJECT** on her arm. Krista. A confession you had to believe. In spite of which her relatives continued devoting themselves to denial *(so that the air must rub its way through instead of exploding through a complete obstruction)* for many years. It was clearly a symptom, but no one knew of what. The boys were busy provoking modifications in her consciousness by acting on certain surfaces of her body *(the distinction between a meaningful word and its meaningless parts is important)* while she distracted herself by considering the notion that since reality **A BASTARD EXISTENCE** could not be proven absolutely *(the sounds apparently lacked such aspiration)* then perhaps this pain did not exist. If a tree falls in a forest and the neighbors turn a blind eye... You know, that awkward stage of phenomenology. Is it the ambiguity *(lost in several dialects)* inherent in words referring to private sensations *(any identity would be purely coincidental)* such as 'pleasure' and 'pain' **CONCERNING WHICH WE CAN NOT SAY WHETHER IT EXISTS** that accounts for her mistaking one for the other

IN FACT OR THEORY and even, at times, equating them? Can her **SENSATION IS** belief that greater abrasion equals greater pleasure *(acoustically distinct, they do not serve to distinguish one word from another)* be chalked up to **A PURE DAYDREAM OF** definition? And, if so, does this explain how she subscribed to such a belief *(so conventionalized as to be unrecognizable as such)* when all of her sensations directly and indisputably **THE PSYCHOLOGIST** refuted it?

That the senses sometimes lie is hardly a new idea, but **WE LEARNED THAT BY ACTING ON** the ability to ignore or misinterpret them *(so we use the same symbol for both)* to the point of endangering **CERTAIN SENSES** one's own safety **WE 'PROVOKE A MODIFICATION'** and well-being **IN THE CONSCIOUSNESS OF THE OTHER** is a technique the fledgling science of psychology has yet to explain. How can the nervous system deceive itself? Under normal circumstances, "no" or "stop" *(sounds for which the alphabet made no provisions)* would be a fit translation of **WE LEARNED THIS** "aversion" but, then, if the stick looks bent **THROUGH LANGUAGE** chances are *(the flow of breath is actually stopped for a split second)* the water flows according to the index of refraction. And, since everyone's experimented on at birth, it simply isn't possible to scrape together a control group *(in speech with a relatively fast tempo, assimilation is quite common)* for the purpose of defining "normal". The trouble seems to have stemmed not from the synapses but from the word "sexuality," about which much was said but little known. Her perception *(taken over and assigned a different value)* of her impulses was forced into alignment with **THAT IS, THROUGH** a lexicon gleaned from those old standard fantasies *(retained in spelling due to conservatism)* which had by default passed into public domain to disguise themselves as private longings while **THE MEANINGFUL AND OBJECTIVE** misogyny and homophobia **REACTIONS OF THE OTHER** raked in the residuals.

$Xq28^1$

1 The "gay gene"[2] which made its debut in the 1990's pertains only to male homosexuality. While studies of twins and patterns of inherited harassment do indicate a biological basis for what Monique Wittig, in "The Straight Mind," refers to as a rejection of the terms of the heterosexual contract, no genetic marker for what is more generally known as "lesbianism" has been found. Or sought. The paucity of knowledge concerning the ratio of biological to cultural factors contributing to female homosexuality is often attributed to the dearth of studies taking women as their subjects, but if, as Wittig says, lesbians are not women, it may

have as much to do with the fact that no one knows exactly which population to study.[6] It is, therefore, unlikely that any advances will be made until the heterosexual infrastructure[7] of the category "women,"[8] and its influence on the endocrine system, is more fully understood. Unfortunately, this is of little concern to those working on the human genome project, although preliminary research by semioticians indicates that stereotypes, as much as genotypes, play a decisive role in mapping complex traits such as sexual orientation.[8] While numerous experiments have demonstrated that narratives have the ability to bond tightly with strands of DNA,[9] thereby producing ideological mutations, the exact mechanisms by which these paradigms exert their effects on the economic ramifications of sexual preferences are, at present, unclear.

2 A misnomer: no such gene was actually identified. Rather, its existence is a probability[3] thought to reside on the very tip of the long arm of the X chromosome in a region containing some 200 codes of conduct.

3 Usually defined as statistically significant obedience to faulty premises encoded at the very tip of the tongue in a spidery mass of canonical threads, waiting to be copied, letter by letter, into experience.

4 A tedious process with only a one-in-a-million chance of finding the intended meaning on the long, twisted strands of historical uncertainty. As women tend to display a wider variety of oppressions[11] and, consequently, linguistic adaptation, than do men, specifying the role of individual enzymes[5] in regulating sexual expression will require more effort than it did in the male project.

---

5 (It has been proposed that, by releasing abnormal amounts of shame, fear, and other unknown byproducts of several centuries, when no one knew what that word meant, into the trachea, they render one completely silent before the final message is encrypted and then brought to trial.)

6 Furthermore, the presence of female homosexuality (quite likely to have existed in oral form long before the destruction of these manuscripts[9]) can only be detected through ambiguous synthetic messages,[4] and while there is a better than 99% chance that the observed identities are real,[3] the insertion or deletion of a single letter can set into play a monotonous sequence of denials regarding the exact nature of the relation which are then

transmitted from one generation to the next. The effects of this on the formation of dignity and happiness can be calamitous, although such errors of omission may prove beneficial to the organism in hostile environments.

7   Originating in the earliest discursive stages, and now in an advanced state of decay, it directs most of our unconscious processes, such as breathing, heart rate, blinking, sexual harassment, marriage, internal temperature, and the continual growth and multiplication of all manner of double standards.[11]

8 A dense, fibrous tissue[7] which must be bathed in a socioeconomic division of the sexes —
folded, thanks to a sort of molecular origami, neatly inside the nucleus of every family — for
normal development to occur.[10] Anticipating the evolution of modern forms of misogyny
which have come to bear a convincing resemblance to feminism, experts have long advised
regular exercise of subtle forms of sexual dimorphism lest the muscle grow flaccid and lose
its definition.

9 (While the spines are relatively durable, the information stored within can be banned[10] at any time.)

10 This process is known as *indoctrination*: traditions normally stored in the form of two vines wrapped around the status quo separate in order to guarantee the reproduction and survival of laboriously alienating complacency.

11 The hypothesis that the transmission of human rights is warded off by semantic antibodies secreted along the highly-contested (and historically variable) membrane of the word "human"[12] has become increasingly plausible since it was first articulated over two centuries ago. (See, for example, Wollstonecraft, *Vindication of the Rights of Woman,* 1792. Her

suggestion that females tend to be thought of rather as women than as human creatures has been confirmed in a handful of small-scale studies. Viewed collectively, the data strongly suggests that women are frequent targets of the social body's essentially reactionary immune system. However, as the side effects of perfectly average figures of speech[9] continue to be covered up with a stubbornly cosmetic skepticism, efforts of corrective lexicography have not, to date, received any major funding.)

12 For example, some political scientists have attempted, in blatant disregard of the uncertainty principle, to map the innate capacity for basic legal protections specifically to the Y chromosome. Just as others have tried to explain the evolutionary advantage of flowery diction by showing it to be an estrogenic effect. While such hasty conclusions serve no useful purpose, they have become lodged in the popular imagination[8] for want of any mechanism in the democratic process to remove them.

Unsound

Precarious to balance on the threshold travels with the legible already melting

Precarious   **melting**

         the threshold   the ice
       ———————   **to balance**   ———————
         is thin   travels with me

Already   **on the legible**

Precarious, to balance
on the legible. The ice is thin, already melting. And the threshold travels with me.

INTIMATE CONVERSATIONS

Scattered hues of green do not amount
to a body of water, and yet here we are,
skipping stones on it. Even though
the concept will dissolve when held
against the misty interplay of light
and other, more elusive spectra.
Your most simple observation
speeds across the surface
while I fall back in tangled arcs
of boolean logic. Despite the brilliant
use of friction, it's impossible
to grasp what pours through
each consecutive enclosure.
The contours too complex, the structure
tenuous, like inner feelings,
or the sway of tones enveloping a mood.

THE STRUCTURE OF DETACHMENT

tangled currents, dark
submerging dark

reflections
wave as they tug

at their roots
a few weeds

plucked
from the unsteady

fragile braid, the sensate
strung together, self

within a sheen of self

      the voice
might be a line

that gropes toward
surface

dangling
in the foreground

solids where the gaze
might rest

a raft tossed out
the glittering

thread

Postcard from Aphasia

Here at the unraveled edge of the immediate spills out of its description
floods each word is full of things that open to the archives bleed through
the emulsion. Categories hover like the longed-for respite from experience
continues skidding downhill always out of focus isolates one aspect from
another leaves its bruise on the porosity of time. I take what notes I can but
words are useless in the rain pours down the stairs into another question
overlaps its boundaries spread evenly in all directions.

POSTCARD FROM APHASIA

All the casual
certainties are dangling here
          The distance seems

          a little asymmetrical
My name is a
haphazard shelter
          propped

          on the conditional
it does not keep me
warm Most words
          I do not understand

          their lattice
structure, and the stillness
they extract

PARALLEL MOTION

If rhythm minus time equals shape,
then shape is a ghost, through which
the hours pour and pour; the aftermath
of song. A hand, a knee —
so naming isolates, and touch evades us
line by line. You think
that you are nearing a conclusion
when you're only walking out along the curvature
in phrase. The music is forever
up ahead, out of reach, and experience
has that syncopated feel, as when
the landscape slips a little
under its map. Or is it the brief delay
in imaging which keeps us
slightly to the left of our surroundings.

WITH A DASH ON THE BEACH

That space does not exist in sound
surprises me. It would seem to be
not merely a metaphorical kind of space,
flattened on the page so as to display
the temporal. There is, for instance,
a mysterious stillness one feels
inside the repetition, as if chronology had been
suspended, and this occurs in sound.
Wide spaces open up between the words
when sung, through which you can see
the shore. Inside, you stay seated, motionless,
while outside, the tones, advancing,
set you gently down
inside a feeling of succession.

based on Barbara Guest's "Roses"

SPACE TAKES ON A SKIN

Temporality
is barely audible

beneath the enigmatic
stasis hung in layers

on the walls.
Like water

pouring through the size
and shape of water

suitably engraved.
A murmuring

annexed to silence,
warm to the touch.

Ƨuture

The problem with duration
is that skin is not
so much a partition
as a rail to lean on.
Points arrive at their sentences
in such a way as to seem
to precede them, when in fact
the transfer expires
promptly at ten. I wanted
to stand on the shore, to feel
the cool spray as it crashes,
unimpaired, into continuance.
But here, there are
no sources, only methods:
void touching void
and between them
periodicity's tactile sham. I remember
how she looked, the strain of
nearness and conjecture, then
how realism slanted to its prototype
and so cut short. I remember discord,
vertigo, elision, though
it was not cold that night,
no matter what the carols say —
they were wrong to begin with.

*

stunned in distance
faltered grip

would not engage
would not subside

the ornate
emptiness between particulars

I you he she, uniformly
captured on film

the sprockets
jammed in litigation

absent
understudy to the gist of it

whose web defies
the chronically arranged

    *

Climbing out across the porous
lining of the finite, we might think
the ground secure, when
at any time, a massive resonance
could catch in the girders,
causing the bridge to collapse.
I thought it best to stay
within the interval, to take as truth
the grainy apparition
of a standing wave. But even there
the rocks are slippery
with moss. Though sound is clothed
in matter, its allegiance
curves through previous
devotions to the present
tense of things. We must forego
these landscapes, cede
our wish to fully explain,
as to stop and smell their roses
would take years of research.
Morning or night, for example,
and the list goes on. The plot
careens down the intricate
knots of consequence,
while what is not reflected
in the anthem's rise to fame
withdraws with the tide.

WITHOUT A SYSTEM OF MOVEMENT

1. Resilience

Event is horizon, draped
across tangents of light.
Will we come to it, relieved
and tangible, no longer caring
how much is lost in completion?
Expedient pose, the sheets
pulled back, already
warm with shape. The way formality
relieves one of the strenuous
details of self, and the long
negotiations with foreground
they entail. If we turn down
these provisions, escape
this narrow shelter of modes —

Fate of the undefined:

shifting borders of skin
and breathing

waver in stasis, dissolving
with inarticulate grace

shunned by the plausible, torn
from the dissonant near

and left
leaning into the glissando

      so many versions,
      none of them ours

2. Disposition

It was precarious, and so
we rested on that ledge, agreed
to follow up the stairs,
into the portrait, inhabit
its tidy charades of what comes next.
Were we afraid to look down,
into the pause, the margins
cluttered with apparitional desires?

Beckoning, adjacent, the explicit
follows on the heels
of the explicit. Shifting
threshold of event,
the night a skin
by whose incision
all impressions are absorbed.
Irreparably smooth,
an object washed up on a beach;
the face we'll know forever
from afar. It fixes
the rush of adjacency; it stays
the incomplete —

the constant
shiver of the unportrayed
in steep dissolves

their legs entwined
in only seeming

and the uncollected rushes
past the dam, under the told, eroding
the certainty of what was

CAST

Stuck in the silver
between two rooms

I had thought that definition was a chamber
where ambiguous desires take on shape, the way
a hand will trace its own reflection in pursuit
of perfect forgery. And that this is why
the category of the lesbian is useful. As if without it
I could no more think to kiss her than ignore
that pressure at the edge of my vocabulary.
Or climb down from this hyperbole to find my way
through the complexities of such a statement.

Perhaps the "I" could function as an anchor,
or a frame. Although it binds
one movement to the next, the chord is
She wanted to escape   nothing to hang onto. Notes decay
her own reflection, or   to the fragility of gesture as you reach to touch
she wanted to inhabit it the contours of a face as seen through cloth
and even light slows down when traveling
through the fibrous metaphors
mistaken for the native language of the psyche.

In fact, it is a network of gravel paths
that never hook up in a clearing. All night,
we paced the edges of what looked like
Loose on its hinges   solid ground, deepening the grooves
the exit alludes   instead of repositioning the lines
to itself   by which we'd been partitioned into speech.
and is reversible   Or mapping out a more accommodating
theory of attraction. Soldered to the this/that
scheme of things in which —

    empirically effaced
            or
    exiled from experience and damned for it
            or
    what it's like to be what there is no such thing as

        aporia and
        dissonance and
        fission

How to say, "This picture does not seem
to coincide with my internal sense"
if the mirror has already swung shut behind you?

GENE EXPRESSION

A vocabulary handed

down through letters

twined in nature

nurture's alphabetic double

helixes where opposites

attract a myth

encoded to protect

the public from

the audible expression of

neologies which propagate

recessive points of

view and threaten to

disorient the language

TEMPLATE

in the grammar of gender   her plus her
                            divided by the intransitive
                                positions
slammed shut in redundancy   supine, necks bared
                        and welded
to an ideal   direct objects may not meet
                            directly
even in photomontage   whereby I imagine

                on the verge of / leaves its gash where / as recorded
                in the diary of / scoured of / explicit reference
                casts its shadow on / tomorrow's entry / tarnishes

                an accident was waiting
                                        in the second paragraph
                                        the intimate
                    lay hidden by the
                                        clarity of
                    common sense
                                        these gestures
                    somehow lifting
                                        mere acoustics
                    into meaning
                                        shipped along the usual
                                        trajectories of romance
                    we are braided to
                                        without the math to solve
            what filters to the bottom
                                        coming to rest
                inert between facts

CENTERPIECE

Something prior to articulation
blooms as discord. Say the pure tone
of a less assertive flute. Or say
the fundamental drops off
suddenly into the messy scrawl
along the postcard's edge.
Is there something
buried in the hybrid
testimonies of medium,
skin, and prediction?
Let flute equal raw sensation
and let medium et al
stand in for language
with its veils and chisels.
I thought to find a block of marble
where instead I found an echo
splashing back and forth
between resemblances.

UNSOUND

I could not escape the principle
of dotted lines, which states
that while the present loops
through the amended rhetorics
of fact, the speed is such
that vertigo is trapped
beneath the probability of faith.
In the night, in the chair,
he sits there, he sits tight,
and so on, voice usurped
by the babble of culture.

The guests were informed
of their options: they could either
be adopted by a context
or adopt one. As if
disparity could benefit
from happy couples
seated in an explanation.

It is not the sound itself
that stops our falling, but the way
the definition spreads its ink.
They took their seats
among the sordid fanfare of tradition
and proclaimed themselves
as general. The pitches stacked up
neatly into walls, blotting out
and filling in, and yet
I was afraid of slipping
through a hole in the interpretation.

NOT ACCESS BUT EXPOSURE IS UNLIMITED

Though in perfect agreement
with experiments designed
to reproduce the blind-spots of analyses
which systematically ignore the evidence
of other evidence and justify said ignorance
with the well-documented silencing
of efforts to expose the symbiotic
methods of exclusionary research, corporate
longevity, and various deductible diseases
which have only x amount of time
to comply with the blame-it-on-essence motif
serving to protect the environment
from scrutiny which might reveal the cause
to be a human intervention here laid out
in sixteen chapters of authoritative
innuendo meant to obfuscate the long-term
risks associated with conforming to
a fabricated standard of acceptable
behavior which by now has been implanted
in millions of beneficiaries

HALF-LIFE

This silence is meticulous,
enduring. Touch / don't touch
is what it says, and that is
what we did, blacked out
entire chapters at a time
so we were always partially
submerged in pools of ink —

> *legal by default*
> *in the regime*
> *of connotation*
> *I have tried*
> *to tell you but*
> *my code is broken*
> *clarity has*
> *consequences*
> *so we live*
> *in the ellipses*
> *on the line*
> *where one tongue meets*
> *another, nowhere*
> *crafted into pitch*

Why am I surprised that they
still write us into sickness.
The atmosphere is lined
with odes to information
blatantly detached from any
actuality. Have I not also
sung along.

Biographical Note:

Jennifer Martenson was born in Seattle, spent a number of years in Chicago and now lives in Providence, RI. She works in libraries and is both a musician and a poet. *Unsound* is her first full book.

This book was designed and computer typeset by Rosmarie Waldrop in 10 pt. Palatino with Benquiat Frisky title, half-titles and initials. Printed on 55 lb. Writers' Natural (an acid-free paper), smyth-sewn and glued into paper covers by McNaughton & Gunn in Saline, Michigan. There are 750 copies.